KT-503-888

A SPIDER BOUGHT A BICYCLE

and other poems for young children

Chosen by Michael Rosen
Illustrated by Inga Moore

KINGFISHER

For Geraldine, Joe, Naomi, Eddie, Laura and Isaac

KINGFISHER
An imprint of Kingfisher Publications Plc
New Penderel House, 283-288 High Holborn
London WC1V 7HZ

First published in paperback by Kingfisher 1992

6 8 10 9 7 5

5(5TR)/1098/SC/MA/USW120

Originally published in hardback with colour illustrations
by Kingfisher 1987

This selection copyright © Michael Rosen 1987
Illustrations copyright © Kingfisher Publications Plc 1987
Cover illustration copyright © Nick Maland 1999
The acknowledgements on page 120 constitute an extension
of this copyright page.

All rights reserved. No part of this publication may be reproduced,
stored in a retrieval system or transmitted by any means electronic,
mechanical, photocopying or otherwise, without the
prior permission of the publisher.

A CIP catalogue record for this book is available
from the British Library

ISBN 0 86272 874 6

Printed in Hong Kong / China

Contents

Wake up, Jacob

Wake up, Jacob, day's a breakin',
Peas in the pot and hoe cake's bakin'.

Wake snakes and bite a biscuit!

Bacon's in the pan and coffee's in the pot,
Come on round and get it while it's hot.

Wake snakes and bite a biscuit!

Early in the morning, almost day,
If you don't come soon, gonna throw it all away.

Wake snakes and bite a biscuit!

Anon (USA)

Waking Up

Oh! I have just had such a lovely dream!
And then I woke,
And all the dream went out like kettle-steam,
Or chimney-smoke.

My dream was all about—how funny, though!
I've only just
Dreamed it, and now it has begun to blow
Away like dust.

In it I went—no! in my dream I had—
No, that's not it!
I can't remember, oh, it is *too* bad,
My dream a bit.

But I saw something beautiful, I'm sure—
Then someone spoke,
And then I didn't see it any more,
Because I woke.

Eleanor Farjeon

Happiness

An empty bus
hurtles through the starry night.
Perhaps the driver is singing
and happy because he sings.

Günter Grass

The Rescue

The wind is loud,
The wind is blowing,
The waves are big,
The waves are growing.
What's that? What's that?
A dog is crying,
It's in the sea,
A dog is crying.
His or hers
Or yours or mine?
A dog is crying,
A dog is crying.

Is no one there?
A boat is going,
The waves are big,
A man is rowing,
The waves are big,
The waves are growing.
Where's the dog?
It isn't crying.
His or hers
Or yours or mine?
Is it dying?
Is it dying?

The wind is loud,
The wind is blowing,
The waves are big,
The waves are growing.
Where's the boat?
It's upside down.
And where's the dog,
And must it drown?
His or hers
Or yours or mine?
O, must it drown?
O, must it drown?

Where's the man?
He's on the sand,
So tired and wet
He cannot stand.
And where's the dog?
It's in his hand,
He lays it down
Upon the sand.
His or hers
Or yours or mine?
The dog is mine,
The dog is mine!

So tired and wet
And still it lies.
I stroke its head,
It opens its eyes,
It wags its tail,
So tired and wet.
I call its name,
For it's my pet,
Not his or hers
Or yours, but mine –
And up it gets,
And up it gets!

Ian Serraillier

Eskimo Lullaby

It's my fat baby
I feel in my hood,
Oh, how heavy he is!

When I turn my head
He smiles at me, my baby,
Hidden in my hood,
Oh, how heavy he is!

How pretty he is when he smiles
With his two teeth, like a little walrus!
Oh I like my baby heavy
And my hood full!

Anon (Greenland)

Little One Sleeps

The little one sleeps in its cradle,
I lift the gauze and look a long time, and silently brush
    away flies with my hand.

Walt Whitman

The House of Cards

A house of cards
  Is neat and small:
Shake the table,
  It must fall.

Find the Court cards
  One by one;
Raise it, roof it,
  Now it's done.
Shake the table!
  That's the fun.

Christina Rossetti

14

Sly Mongoose

Sly mongoose
Dog know you ways
Sly mongoose
Dog know you ways
Mongoose went to de master's kitchen
Pick up one of de fattest chicken
Put it in de wais'-coat pocket
Sly mongoose.

Anon (Caribbean)

Quartermaster's Stores

There were rats, rats
running around in hats
in the stores
in the stores.
There were rats, rats
running around in hats
in the Quartermaster's Stores.

My eyes are dim
I cannot see,
I have not brought my specs with me
I have not brought my specs with me.

There were eggs, eggs
running around on legs
in the stores
in the stores.
There were eggs, eggs
running around on legs
in the Quartermaster's Stores.

My eyes are dim
I cannot see,
I have not brought my specs with me
I have not brought my specs with me.

There was cheese, cheese
crawling on its knees
in the stores
in the stores.
There was cheese, cheese
crawling on its knees
in the Quartermaster's Stores.

My eyes are dim
I cannot see,
I have not brought my specs with me
I have not brought my specs with me.

There was jelly, jelly
sliding on its belly
in the stores
in the stores.
There was jelly, jelly
sliding on its belly
in the Quartermaster's Stores.

My eyes are dim
I cannot see,
I have not brought my specs with me
I have not brought my specs with me.

Anon

17

Do You Love Me?

Do you love me
or do you not?
You told me once
but I forgot.

Anon

Roses are Red

Roses are red
violets are blue;
most poems rhyme
this one doesn't.

Anon

Praise Song of the Wind

Trees with weak roots
I will strike, I the wind.
I will roar, I will whistle.

Haycocks built today
I will scatter, I the wind.
I will roar, I will whistle.

Badly made haycocks
I will carry off, I the wind.
I will roar, I will whistle.

Uncovered stacks of sheaves
I will soak through, I the wind.
I will roar, I will whistle.

Houses not tightly roofed
I will destroy, I the wind.
I will roar, I will whistle.

Hay piled in sheds
I will tear apart, I the wind.
I will roar, I will whistle.

Fire kindled in the road
I will set flickering, I the wind.
I will roar, I will whistle.

Houses with bad smoke-holes
I will shake, I the wind.
I will roar, I will whistle.

The farmer who does not think
I will make to think, I the wind.
I will roar, I will whistle.

The worthless slug-a-bed
I will wake, I the wind.
I will roar, I will whistle.

Anon
(Teleut People of Siberia)

Silent Sea

'We were the first that ever burst
Into that silent sea.'

Down dropped the breeze,
   the sails dropped down
'Twas sad as sad could be;
And we did speak only to break
The silence of the sea!

All in a hot and copper sky
The bloody Sun, at noon
Right up above the mast did stand
No bigger than the moon.

Day after day, day after day
We stuck, nor breath nor motion;
As idle as a painted ship
Upon a painted ocean.

Water, water everywhere
And all the boards did shrink;
Water, water everywhere
Nor any drop to drink.

The very deep did rot: Oh Christ!
That ever this should be!
Yea, slimy things did crawl with legs
Upon the slimy sea.

Samuel Taylor Coleridge

from The Tempest

Be not afeared;* the isle is full of noises,
Sounds and sweet airs, that give delight, and hurt not.
Sometimes a thousand twanging instruments
Will hum about mine ears; and sometimes voices,
That, if I then had waked after long sleep,
Will make me sleep again: and then, in dreaming,
The clouds methought would open, and show riches
Ready to drop upon me; that, when I waked,
I cried to dream again.

*afeared = afraid

William Shakespeare

The Panther Roars

The panther roars on the mountain,
The tiger roars in the forest,
The king roars on his throne
With sword and shield in hand.

Anon
(Gond, India)

The Flood

Well, it rained five days
          and the sky was as dark as night.
Yes, it rained five days
          and the sky was as dark as night.
There's trouble in the lowlands tonight.

I got up one morning,
          I couldn't even get out of my door,
I got up one morning,
          I couldn't even get out of my door,
That was enough trouble to make a poor boy
          wonder where to go.

I went and stood up on a high lonesome hill,
I went and stood up on a high lonesome hill,
I did all I could to look down
          on the house where I used to live.

It thundered and it lightninged
          and the wind began to blow.
It thundered and it lightninged
          and the wind began to blow.
There were thousands of poor people
          didn't have no place to go.

Anon (USA)

Captain Cook

Captain Cook made some soup,
His mother made some jelly.
Captain Cook fell in the soup
And burnt a hole in his belly.

Anon (Australia)

One Bath

One bath
after another –
how stupid.

Issa

Bath Time

The boy stood on the burning deck
Washing himself like mad;
He got the soap and rolled it up
And flicked it at his dad.

Anon

The Wicked Postman

Why do you sit there on the floor so quiet and silent, tell me, mother dear?

The rain is coming in through the open window, making you all wet, and you don't mind it.

Do you hear the gong striking four? It is time for my brother to come home from school.

What has happened to you that you look so strange?

Haven't you got a letter from father to-day?

I saw the postman bringing letters in his bag for almost everybody in the town.

Only, father's letters he keeps to read himself. I am sure the postman is a wicked man.

But don't be unhappy about that, mother dear.

To-morrow is market day in the next village. You ask your maid to buy some pens and papers.

I myself will write all father's letters; you will not find a single mistake.

I shall write from A right up to K.

But, mother, why do you smile?

You don't believe that I can write as nicely as father does!

But I shall rule my paper carefully, and write all the letters beautifully big.

When I finish my writing do you think I shall be so foolish as father and drop it into the horrid postman's bag?

I shall bring it to you myself without waiting, and letter by letter help you to read my writing.

I know the postman does not like to give you the really nice letters.

Rabindranath Tagore

There was an Old Lady

There was an old lady who swallowed a fly.
My! My!
Poor old lady, she'll surely die.

There was an old lady who swallowed a spider.
Whoops! It went right down inside her.
She swallowed the spider to eat up the fly.
My! My!
Poor old lady, she'll surely die.

There was an old lady who swallowed a bird.
How absurd! She swallowed a bird.
She swallowed the bird to eat up the spider.
Whoops! It went right down inside her.
She swallowed the spider to eat up the fly.
My! My!
Poor old lady, she'll surely die.

There was an old lady who swallowed a cat.
Fancy that! She swallowed a cat.
She swallowed the cat to eat up the bird.
How absurd! She swallowed a bird.
She swallowed the bird to eat up the spider.
Whoops! It went right down inside her.
She swallowed the spider to eat up the fly.
My! My!
Poor old lady, she'll surely die.

There was an old lady who swallowed a dog.
The hog! To swallow a dog.
She swallowed the dog to eat up the cat.
Fancy that! She swallowed a cat.
She swallowed the cat to eat up the bird.
How absurd! She swallowed a bird.
She swallowed the bird to eat up the spider.
Whoops! It went right down inside her.
She swallowed the spider to eat up the fly.
My! My!
Poor old lady, she'll surely die.

There was an old lady who swallowed a cow.
How now! She swallowed a cow.
She swallowed the cow to eat up the dog.
The hog! She swallowed a dog.
She swallowed the dog to eat up the cat.
Fancy that! She swallowed a cat.
She swallowed the cat to eat up the bird.
How absurd! She swallowed a bird.
She swallowed the bird to eat up the spider.
Whoops! It went right down inside her.
She swallowed the spider to eat up the fly.
My! My!
Poor old lady, she'll surely die.

There was an old lady
who swallowed a horse.
She died of course.

Two Pilots

Two pilots went up in an aeroplane
The aeroplane had a good engine.
That's good.
No, that's bad. The engine stopped.
Oh, that's bad.
No, they had parachutes.
Oh, that's good.
No, that was bad – the parachutes
        didn't open.
Oh, that was bad.
No, there was a lake under them.
Oh, that's good.
No, that was bad. There was
        a crocodile in the lake.
Oh, that's bad.
No, no, they missed the crocodile.
Oh, that's good.
No, that was bad.
Why?
They missed the lake.
Oh!

Adapted by Michael Rosen

BED!

When it is time to go to bed
my mum says:
'BED!'
I say:
'Please can I stay up
until this film finishes?'
'What time does it finish?'
        my mum says.
'Ten o'clock,' I say.
'No way,' my mum says.
'Oh can't I stay up for five minutes?'
'NO.'
'Please.'
'NO!'
'Oh . . . can't I read in bed?'
'NO!'
'Please.'
'Come here, girl . . . You are getting on my nerves
if you are not in that bed
by the time I count to . . .'

I walk slowly up the stairs
my brother is laughing away.
Then my mum starts shouting again.
This time at my brother.

Joni Akinrele

Miss Mary

Miss Mary	she asked her	He jumped so
Mack	mother	high
Mack	mother	high
Mack	mother	high
all dressed in	for fifty	he reached the
black	cents	sky
black	cents	sky
black	cents	sky
with silver	to watch the	he didn't come
buttons	elephant	down
buttons	elephant	down
buttons	elephant	down
all down her	jump the	till the fifth of Ju-
back	fence	ly
back	fence	ly
back	fence.	ly.

Anon (USA)

When I was Small

When I was small
the wall was tall.
But now I'm tall
the wall looks small.

Jay Reed

My Bonnie

My Bonnie lies over the ocean,
My Bonnie lies over the sea,
My Bonnie lies over the ocean;
Oh bring back my Bonnie to me.

Bring back, Bring back,
Oh bring back my Bonnie to me, to me.
Bring back, Bring back,
Oh bring back my Bonnie to me.

Oh blow ye winds over the ocean,
Oh blow ye winds over the sea,
Oh blow ye winds over the ocean
And bring back my Bonnie to me.

Last night as I lay on my pillow,
Last night as I lay on my bed,
Last night as I lay on my pillow
I dreamed my poor Bonnie was dead.

The winds have blown over the ocean,
The winds have blown over the sea,
The winds have blown over the ocean
And brought back my Bonnie to me.

Anon

I've a Lordy in America

I've a lordy in America,
I've a lordy in Dundee-i-ee (i-ee, i-ee, i),
I've a lordy in Australia
and he's coming here to marry me (i-ee, i-ee).

First he took me for my wedding dress,
Then he took me for my tea (i-ee, i-ee, i-ee, i),
Then he ran away and left me
with my three bonny babes on my knee (i-ee, i-ee).

One was sitting on the fire-place
One was sitting on my knee (i-ee, i-ee, i-ee, i)
One was sitting on my doorstep
saying, 'Daddy, daddy, daddy, come to me (i-ee, i-ee).'

Anon

My Old Man's a Dustman

My old man's a dustman
he wears a dustman's hat
he bought two thousand tickets
to see a football match.

Fatty passed to Skinny
Skinny passed it back
Fatty took a rotten shot
and knocked the goalie flat.

Where was the goalie
when the ball was in the net?
Half way up the goalpost
with his trousers round his neck.

Singing:
umpah umpah
stick it up your jumper
rule Britannia
marmalade and jam
we threw sausages at our old man.

They put him on the stretcher
they put him on the bed
they rubbed his belly
with a five pound jelly
but the poor old soul was dead.

Anon

The Common Cormorant

The common cormorant or shag
Lays eggs inside a paper bag
The reason you will see no doubt
It is to keep the lightning out.
But what these unobservant birds
Have never noticed is that herds
Of wandering bears may come with buns
And steal the bags to hold the crumbs.

Anon

A Wise Old Owl

A wise old owl sat in an oak,
The more he heard, the less he spoke;
The less he spoke, the more he heard.
Why aren't we all like that wise old bird?

Anon

Space Shuttle

Monday
my Aunt Esmeralda
gave me one of those
s p a c e - h o p p e r s .
You know,
those big orange things
that you sit on and
they're supposed to take you to the s$_t$a^r^{s}$^.$
Didn't take me any further than
the lamp-post –
and that hurt.

Tuesday
I gave it to my baby brother.
Do you know, he really believes
it's going to work!
Some people will believe
anything.

Friday.
Just had a postcard
from my brother.
From the moon.
It says
'Had a good journey.
See you soon.
Just hopping off to M^{a}r$_s$$^!$

Judith Nicholls

Office Cleaner

You can recognise an office cleaner
by the scarf on her head.
If she hasn't got a scarf
you'll see her shopping bag.
You'll see her
just drowsing along
because she's weary.

She has gotten up
about 6 in the morning
and has been to the public baths
to do her washing and ironing
and rushed home.
Then she has gone out
to do her shopping
and gone home again
to give her children their dinner
if they don't stay at school.
Now she's hurrying back
to give her husband his dinner.

Annie Spike

The German Measles

I had the German measles
I had them very bad.
They wrapped me in a blanket
And put me in a van.

The van was very bumpy
And I nearly tumbled out
And when I got to hospital
I heard a baby shout:

'Mamma, dadda, take me home,
from this little rusty home.
I've been here a year or two
and oh I want to stay with you.'

Here comes a doctor. Doctor Brown
Asking questions all around:
'Are you ill, or are you not?'
'Yes I am, you silly clot.'

Here comes Doctor
                Glannister
sliding down the bannister.
Halfway down he ripped
                his pants
and now he's doing
          a cha-cha dance.

Anon

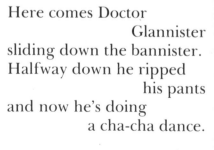

44

Miss Polly

Miss Polly had a dolly
who was sick, sick, sick.
So she sent for the doctor
to come quick, quick, quick.
The doctor came
with his bag and his hat
and he knocked at the door
with a rat-a-tat-tat.
He looked at the dolly
and he shook his head
and he said, 'Miss Polly,
put her straight to bed.'
He wrote down on a paper
for a pill, pill, pill.
'I'll be back in the morning
with the bill, bill, bill.'

Anon

Old Doc Hare

An old Hare lived in a house on a hill,
One hundred years old and never was ill;
His ears so long and his eyes so big,
And his legs so spry that he danced a jig;
He lived so long that he knew everything
About the beasts that walk and the birds that sing—
      This old Doc Hare,
      Who lived up there
In a mighty fine house on a mighty high hill.

He was doctor for all the beasts and birds—
He put on his specs and he used big words,
He felt the pulse, then he looked mighty wise,
He pulled out his watch and he shut both eyes;
He grabbed up his hat and he grabbed up his cane,
Then—'blam' went the door—he was gone like a train,
      This old Doc Hare,
      Who lived up there
In a mighty fine house on a mighty high hill.

Mister Bear fell sick—they sent for Doc Hare,
'Oh, Doctor, come quick, and see Mr Bear;
He's mighty near dead just as sure as you're born!
Too much of young pig, too much of green corn.'
As he put on his hat, said old Doc Hare:
'I'll take along my lance and lance Mister Bear,'
               Said old Doc Hare,
               Who lived up there
In a mighty fine house on a mighty high hill.

Mister Bear he groaned, Mister Bear he growled,
While the old Mrs Bear and the children howled,
Doctor Hare took out his sharp little lance,
And pierced Mister Bear till it made him prance,

Then he grabbed up his hat and grabbed up his cane—
'Blam' went the door, he was gone like a train,
               This old Doc Hare,
               Who lived up there
In a mighty fine house on a mighty high hill.

James Edwin Campbell

47

Apple Tree

Apple-tree, apple-tree,
Bear apples for me:
Hats full, laps full
Sacks full, caps full:
Apple-tree, apple-tree,
Bear apples for me.

Anon (England)

Into the Kitchen

Into the kitchen
Sulin goes
With a chicken
And potatoes.

She puts some water
Into a pot
Then she waits
Until it's hot.

Into the pot
She puts the chicken,
While it cooks
The soup will thicken.

She adds the potatoes
And stirs the pot,
When everything's cooked
She'll eat it hot.

Patricia Maria Tan

Jelly on the Plate

Jelly on the plate
jelly on the plate
wibble wobble
wibble wobble
jelly on the plate.

Sausage in the pan
sausage in the pan
sizzle sizzle
sizzle sizzle
sausage in the pan.

Sweeties in the jar
sweeties in the jar
pick them out
eat them up
sweeties in the jar.

Burglar in the house
burglar in the house
chuck him out
chuck him out
burglar in the house.

50

Apples on the tree
apples on the tree
pick them off
pick them off
apples on the tree.

Baby on the floor
baby on the floor
pick it up
pick it up
baby on the floor.

Ants in your pants
ants in your pants
scratch them off
scratch them off
ants in your pants.

Ice cream in the fridge
ice cream in the fridge
FREEZE!

Anon

51

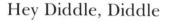

Hey Diddle, Diddle

Hey diddle, diddle,
The cat and the fiddle,
The cow jumped
                over the moon;
The little dog laughed
To see such fun,
And the dish ran away

with the chocolate biscuits

Traditional,
adapted by Michael Rosen

Who Ate the Cakes?

Adam
had 'em.

Anon

Poor Meatball

On top of spaghetti
all covered with cheese,
I lost my poor meatball
when somebody sneezed.

It rolled off the table
and onto the floor.
And then my poor meatball
rolled out of the door.

It rolled out in the garden
and under a bush.
And then my poor meatball
got covered in slush.

So if you have spaghetti
all covered in cheese,
Hold on to your meatball
'cos somebody might sneeze.

Anon

Upside-down Cake

I am going to make
An upside-down cake.
I know I'll need some flour,
But I'm going to wait
At least half an hour
Before I begin to bake.

I'll need some fat
And eggs, and water,
Sugar in an upside-down bowl
And mix all of that.

Before I can really begin
I'll need an upside-down tin,
And an upside-down oven
To fit everything in.

I know you will say
I will have to stand on my head
To eat an upside-down cake.
But I have thought of that:
I will choke and be dead.

So I will change my mind
And bake instead
A sideways cake
And eat it
Sideways in bed.

I. Choonara

Minnie

I went downtown
To meet Mrs Brown.
She gave me a nickel
To buy me a pickle.
The pickle was sour
She gave me a flower
The flower was dead
She gave me a thread
The thread was thin
She gave me a pin
The pin was sharp
She gave me a harp
The harp began to sing
Minnie and a minnie and a ha, ha, ha.

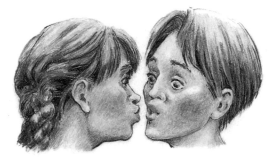

Minnie and a minnie and a ha, ha, ha,
Kissed her fellow in a trolley car.
I told Ma, Ma told Pa.
Minnie got a licking and a ha, ha, ha.

Anon (USA)

Down to the River

Went down to the river
heard a mighty racket.
Nothing but the bull-frog
pulling off his jacket

Anon (USA)

A Spider Bought a Bicycle

A spider bought a bicycle
And had it painted black
He started off along the road
with an earwig on his back
He sent the pedals round so fast
he travelled all the day
Then he took the earwig off
And put the bike away.

Phyllis Kingsbury

The Good Little Girl

It's funny how often they say to me, 'Jane?
    Have you been a *good* girl?'
    'Have you been a *good* girl?'
And when they have said it, they say it again,
    'Have you been a *good* girl?'
    'Have you been a *good* girl?'

I go to a party, I go out to tea,
I go to an aunt for a week at the sea,
I come back from school or from playing a game;
Wherever I come from, it's always the same:
    'Well?
Have you been a *good* girl, Jane?'

It's always the end of the loveliest day:
    'Have you been a *good* girl?'
    'Have you been a *good* girl?'
I went to the Zoo, and they waited to say:
    'Have you been a *good* girl?'
    'Have you been a *good* girl?'

Well, what did they think that I went there to do?
And why should I want to be bad at the Zoo?
And should I be likely to say if I had?
So that's why it's funny of Mummy and Dad,
This asking and asking, in case I was bad,
    'Well?
    Have you been a *good* girl, Jane?'

                    A. A. Milne

Three Girls

There were once three girls
all in the same bed.
It was so crowded
one of them had to get out,
and she tried to sleep on the floor.

After a while
one of the girls left in the bed said:
'Come back in the bed
there's more room now.'

Anon, adapted by
Michael Rosen

The Mouse's Lullaby

Oh, rock-a-by, baby mouse, rock-a-by, so!
When baby's asleep to the baker's I'll go,
And while he's not looking I'll pop from a hole,
And bring to my baby a fresh penny roll.

Palmer Cox

London Bridge

London Bridge is falling down,
Falling down, falling down,
London Bridge is falling down,
My hairy baby.

adapted by Michael Rosen

Mary's gone A-milking

Mary's gone a-milking,
gentle sweet mother of mine.

Take your pails and go after her,
gentle sweet daughter of mine.

Buy me a pair of new milking pails,
gentle sweet mother of mine.

Where's the money to come from,
gentle sweet daughter of mine?

Sell my father's feather bed,
gentle sweet mother of mine.

What's your father to sleep on,
gentle sweet daughter of mine?

Put him in the truckle bed,
gentle sweet mother of mine.

What are the children to sleep on,
gentle sweet daughter of mine?

Put them in the pig sty,
gentle sweet mother of mine.

What are the pigs to lie in,
gentle sweet daughter of mine?

Put them in the washing tubs,
gentle sweet mother of mine.

What am I to wash in,
gentle sweet daughter of mine?

Wash in the river,
gentle sweet mother of mine.

Suppose the clothes should blow away,
gentle sweet daughter of mine?

Set a man to watch them,
gentle sweet mother of mine.

Suppose the man should go to sleep,
gentle sweet daughter of mine?

Take a boat and go after them,
gentle sweet mother of mine.

Suppose the boat should be upset,
gentle sweet daughter of mine?

Then that would be the end of you,
gentle sweet mother of mine.

Anon

Cows

Half the time they munched the grass, and all
      the time they lay
Down in the water-meadows, the lazy month of May,
    A-chewing,
    A-mooing,
  To pass the hours away.

  'Nice weather,' said the brown cow.
    'Ah,' said the white.
  'Grass is very tasty.'
    'Grass is all right.'

Half the time they munched the grass, and all
      the time they lay
Down in the water-meadows, the lazy month of May,
    A-chewing,
    A-mooing,
  To pass the hours away.

  'Rain coming,' said the brown cow.
    'Ah,' said the white.
    'Flies is very tiresome.'
    'Flies bite.'

Half the time they munched the grass, and all
        the time they lay
Down in the water-meadows, the lazy month of May,
    A-chewing,
    A-mooing,
  To pass the hours away.

  'Time to go,' said the brown cow.
    'Ah,' said the white.
  'Nice chat.' 'Very pleasant.'
    'Night.' 'Night.'

Half the time they munched the grass, and all
        the time they lay
Down in the water-meadows, the lazy month of May,
    A-chewing,
    A-mooing,
  To pass the hours away.

James Reeves

If I was a Bird . . .

If I was a bird
I would like to fly in the sky
so that everyone could see me.
I could fly in and out of the clouds and caves.
There'd be just one pest in my life –
that's a man with a gun to shoot me.
Him I wouldn't like.

If I was a man and not a bird,
I'd never shoot at birds
because a bird is lovely to see
when it's flying.
If I was a man I'd just watch,
not shoot.

Anon

Brothers over the Sea

I had two brothers over the sea,
And they both sent a present unto me.

The first sent a goose without a bone;
The second sent a cherry without a stone.

How can there be a goose without a bone?
How can there be a cherry without a stone?

When the goose is in the egg-shell, there is no bone;
When the cherry's in the blossom, there is no stone.

Anon (England)

Frozen-out Gardeners

We're broken-hearted gardeners,
        scarce got a bit of shoe;
Like pilgrims we are wandering
        and we don't know what to do.
In summer time the leaves upon
        the trees appear so green;
In autumn they do fade and fall
        and none are to be seen.
The hollyhock, the dahlia, the lily, pink and rose,
The turnips and the cabbages are all together froze.
Cold winter it is come at last and we are all froze out.
Our furniture is seized upon,
        our togs are up the spout.
These times they are so very hard
        and the winter winds do blow:
Oh think upon the poor folk
        in the bitter frost and snow.

Anon (19th century)

When I went Out

When I went out to see the sun
There wasn't sun or anyone
But there was only sand and sea
And lots of rain that fell on me
And where the rain and river met
The water got completely wet.

Karla Kuskin

Lament

Listen, children:
Your father is dead.
From his old coats
I'll make you little jackets;
I'll make you little trousers
From his old pants.
There'll be in his pockets
Things he used to put there,
Keys and pennies
Covered with tobacco;
Dan shall have the pennies
To save in his bank;
Anne shall have the keys
To make a pretty noise with.
Life must go on,
And the dead be forgotten;
Life must go on,
Though good men die;
Anne, eat your breakfast;
Dan, take your medicine;
Life must go on;
I forget just why.

Edna St Vincent Millay

Sometimes

Sometimes I feel like a motherless child
Sometimes I feel like a motherless child
A long way from home.

Sometimes I feel like a feather in the air
Sometimes I feel like a feather in the air
A long way from home.

Anon (USA)

Ellery my Son

Where have you been all the day,
Ellery my son?
Where have you been all the day,
my beloved one?
Out, dear mother,
Out, dear mother.
Oh Mother dear, come quick,
I feel sick, very sick
And I wanna lay down and die.

What did you there,
Ellery my son?
What did you there,
my beloved one?
Ate, dear mother,
Ate, dear mother.
Oh Mother dear,
                come quick,
I feel sick, very sick
And I wanna lay down
                and die.

What did you eat,
Ellery my son?
What did you eat,
my beloved one?
Eels, mother,
Eels, mother.
Oh Mother dear, come quick,
I feel sick, very sick
And I wanna lay down and die.

What colour were they,
Ellery my son?
What colour were they,
my beloved one?
Green and yella,
Green and yella.
Oh Mother dear, come quick,
I feel sick, very sick
And I wanna lay down and die.

Them eels was snakes,
Ellery my son.
Them eels was snakes,
My beloved one.
Yuk, dear mother,
Yuk, dear mother.
Oh Mother dear, come quick,
I feel sick, very sick
And I wanna lay down and die.

Anon

My Mum Said

My mum said to me and my brother:
'Don't crumble your bread or roll in the soup.'
I said:
'I don't want to roll in my soup.'

Then she said:
'Eat up, Michael.'
And my brother said:
'I don't want to eat up Michael.'

Michael Rosen

Over the Garden Wall

Over the garden wall
I let my baby fall.
My mother came out
she gave me a clout
over the garden wall.

Over the garden wall
I let my baby fall.
My mother came out
she gave me a clout
she asked me what
it was all about
over the garden wall.

Over the garden wall
I let my baby fall.
My mother came out
she gave me a clout
she gave me another
to match the other
over the garden wall.

Anon

Little by Little

In England they say:
Little drops of water
make the mighty ocean.

In France they say:
Little by little
the bird makes his nest.

In Spain they say:
Little by little
the cup is filled.

In Japan they say:
Dust can pile up
to make a mountain.

In Arabic people say:
A hair from here
and a hair from there
makes a beard.

In Germany they say:
Many drops of water
dripping onto a stone
can make a hole in it.

Michael Rosen

The Walk

One day a man took a walk.

One day a man took a walk with his friend.

One day a man took a walk with his friend and his dog.

One day a man took a walk with his friend and his dog. The dog wore a red jacket.

One day a man took a walk with his friend and his dog. The dog wore a red jacket with polka dots.

One day a man took a walk with his friend and his dog. The dog wore a red jacket with polka dots. The dog was hungry.

One day a man took a walk with his friend and his dog. The dog wore a red jacket with polka dots. The dog was hungry so he bit his master.

One day a man took a walk with his friend and his dog. The dog wore a red jacket with polka dots. The dog was hungry so he bit his master. The master got angry.

One day a man took a walk with his friend and his dog. The dog wore a red jacket with polka dots. The dog was hungry so he bit his master. The master got angry and he bit him back.

Anon (USA)

The Day our Dog Died

It was Sunday morning when I awoke
To see the face of my mum.
She, her eyes full of tears, said
Softly, unsteadily, 'She . . . She's
Gone in her sleep.'
I felt upset, yet in a way
Happy—
For she was blind and almost deaf
But full of life.
It seemed a cruel kind of thing,
Like one of the family had died.
I waited until my mum had gone,
And for a while cried.
I went downstairs, my head aching
And my dog gone.

Ramona Harris

Weep Weep

weep weep
then sleep
deep deep

Anon (USA)

Dream Variations

To fling my arms wide,
In some place of the sun,
To whirl and to dance
Till the white day is done,
Then rest at cool evening
Beneath a tall tree
While night comes on gently,
    Dark like me,—
That is my dream!

To fling my arms wide,
In the face of the sun,
Dance! whirl! whirl!
Till the quick day is done,
Rest at pale evening. . .
A tall, slim tree. . .
Night coming tenderly,
    Black like me.

Langston Hughes

The Gentle Giant

Every night
At twelve o'clock,
The gentle giant
Takes a walk;
With a cry cried high
And a call called low,
The gentle giant
Walks below.

    And as he walks,
    He cries, he calls:

'Bad men, boogie men,
Bully men, shoo!
No one in the neighbourhood
Is scared of you.
The children are asleep,
And the parents are too:
Bad men, boogie men,
Bully men, shoo!'

        Dennis Lee

Tracy, our Teacher, Telling us to go Out

'Come on, out to play you lot.
Come on, Hafiza, no time to waste.'

'But Miss . . .'

'No, Hafiza.
Come on, Elie, you heard what I said,
so COME ON.
Come on, Emma, you can do that
afterwards. . .
. . . Emma!'

'Ohh, what was that?'

'GO OUT!'

'Sorry, Tracy, I was too busy doing my work.'

'Come on, Pearl. Out to play, PEARL.
Are you deaf, or something?'

'Wait a minute, Tracy.'

'Pearl, out you go.'

'OK.'

'Theresa, there's no time to hug Mark,
out you go.
Come on, Sara, put that away
and go out.'

So we did go out
and anyway
it's not fair
all the teachers stay in
while we go outside.

It's really boring.

Elie Bagum

Our Joe

Our Joe wants to know
if your Joe will lend our Joe your Joe's banjo.
If your Joe won't lend our Joe
your Joe's banjo,
our Joe won't lend your Joe
our Joe's banjo
when our Joe has a banjo!

Anon

Spelling Difficulty

Mrs D
Mrs I
Mrs FFI
Mrs C
Mrs U
Mrs LTY

Anon

The Underground Train

Once you get on the underground train
The people stare at you.
Their eyes
seem to be glued on you
From the moment you get on the train
until the moment you get off the train
Their eyes look like bronze
No one speaks
They all stay quiet and still
You try to stop looking at them
But you can't
Then some of them look up
At the posters on the roof
But they soon stare back at you again.
The train stops
Suddenly there is a buzz of conversation
At last you are out
You feel much better.

Jayne Spooner

Animal Fair

I went to the animal fair,
All the birds and the beasts were there,
The gay baboon by the light of the moon
Was combing his yellow hair.
The monkey fell from his bunk
And slid down the elephant's trunk.
The elephant sneezed, and fell on his knees
And what became of the mon-key,
    mon-key, mon-key, mon-key,
    monkey?

Anon

Turn Around

I was going to the country
going to the fair
when I met the senorita
with the curl in her hair.
Shake, senorita,
shake it all you can.
Shake, senorita,
till you find a handsome man.
Rumble to the bottom
rumble to the top
turn around
turn around
turn around
stop.

Anon

Dudley Market, 1827

At Dudley Market now I tell
Most kinds of articles they sell:
Hats, caps and bonnets blue
And trousers wide enough for two,
Rocking chairs and children's cradles,
Porridge pots and wooden ladles.
There's butter, bacon, cheese and eggs
Sold by Old Giles with crooked legs.
There's plum pudding, both rich and nice
On the next stall, tuppence a slice.
There's one-armed Joe among the lot
With mutton pies all smoking hot.
Please to remember what I am sayin'
You will never hear the like again.

Ben Boucher

Truro Agricultural Show

There's things up there that'll make you laugh;
There's a two-legged cow and a nine-legged calf,
A billy-goat that comes from Wales
With sixteen eyes and seventeen tails.

Anon (England)

Man in a Hurry

He was a man in a hurry
from the day he was born.
He had to go to market
at the break of dawn.

He put on his wife's green trousers
and off he went to town,
sitting on his donkey
the wrong way round.

Chinese nursery rhyme,
adapted by Michael Rosen

Hello, Sir

Hello, sir, hello, sir,
Meet you at the show, sir.
No, sir. Why, sir?
Because I've got a cold, sir.

Where'd you get the cold, sir?
At the north pole, sir.
What were you doing there, sir?
Catching polar bears, sir.

How many did you catch, sir?
One sir, two sir, three sir, four sir, five sir,
Six sir, seven sir, eight sir, nine sir, ten sir.
All the rest were dead, sir.

How did they die, sir?
Eating apple pie, sir.
What was in the pie, sir?
A big fat fly, sir.

What was in the fly, sir?
A big fat germ, sir.
What was in the germ, sir?
A big fat you, sir!

Anon (Australia)

The Skyfoogle

There was a man
who turned up round our way once
put up a tent in the park, he did,
put up notices all round the streets saying
that he was going to put on show
A TERRIFYING CREATURE!!!!!!
called:
THE SKYFOOGLE!!!!!!!
No one had ever seen this thing before.
The show was on for
2 o'clock, the next day.

Next day, we all turned up to see
THE FIERCEST ANIMAL IN THE WORLD!!!!!!!!!
The man took the money at the door.
And we poured into the tent.
There was a kind of stage up one end
with a curtain in front of it.
We all sat down and waited.
The man went off behind the curtain.
Suddenly we heard a terrible scream.
There was an awful yelling and crying,
there was the noise of chains rattling
and someone shouting.
Suddenly the man came running
                    on to the stage
in front of the curtain.
All his clothes were torn,
there was blood on his face
and he screamed:

Quick, get out
get out
get out of here,
THE SKYFOOGLE HAS ESCAPED!!!!!!!

We got up
and ran out the door
and got away as fast as we could.

By the time we got ourselves together
the man had gone.
We never saw him again.
We never saw our money again either . . .
. . . And none of us has ever seen
          THE SKYFOOGLE!!!!!

Traditional,
adapted by Michael Rosen

They all Went

Once upon a time
the cat drank wine
the monkey chewed tobacco
on the street car line.
The line broke
the monkey got choked
and they all went to heaven
in a little row boat.

Anon (USA)

Och-a-nee

Och-a-nee
when I was wee
I used to sit
on my granny's knee:
Her apron tore
I fell on the floor.
Och-a-nee
when I was wee.

Anon (Scotland)

Waiting at the Window

These are my two drops of rain
Waiting on the window-pane.

I am waiting here to see
Which the winning one will be.

Both of them have different names.
One is John and one is James.

All the best and all the worst
Comes from which of them is first.

James had just begun to ooze.
He's the one I want to lose.

John is waiting to begin.
He's the one I want to win.

James is going slowly on.
Something sort of sticks to John.

John is moving off at last.
James is going pretty fast.

John is rushing down the pane.
James is going slow again.

James has met a sort of smear.
John is getting very near.

Is he going fast enough?
(James has found a piece of fluff.)

John has hurried quickly by.
(James was talking to a fly.)

John is there, and John has won!
Look! I told you! Here's the sun!

                              A. A. Milne

Allie

'Allie, call the birds in,
The birds from the sky.'
Allie calls, Allie sings,
Down they all fly.
First there came
Two white doves
Then a sparrow from his nest,
Then a clucking bantam hen,
Then a robin red-breast.

'Allie, call the beasts in,
The beasts, every one.'
Allie calls, Allie sings,
In they all run.
First there came
Two black lambs,
Then a grunting Berkshire sow,
Then a dog without a tail,
Then a red and white cow.

'Allie, call the fish up,
The fish from the stream.'
Allie calls, Allie sings,
Up they all swim.
First there came
Two gold fish,
A minnow and a miller's thumb,
Then a pair of loving trout,
Then the twisted eels come.

'Allie, call the children,
Children from the green.'
Allie calls, Allie sings,
Soon they run in.
First there came
Tom and Madge,
Kate and I who'll not forget
How we played by the water's edge
Till the April sun set.

Robert Graves

What's your Name?

What's your name?
Johnny Maclean.
Where do you live?
Down the lane.
What's your shop?
Lollypop.
What's your number?
Cucumber.

What's your name?
Mary Jane.
Where do you live?
Cabbage Lane.
What's your number?
Rain and thunder.
What address?
Watercress.

Anon

Why?

When the vase gets broken,
          why do I always get the blame?
When the garden's untidy,
          why do I have to clear it up?
When the book gets ripped,
          why do I have to mend it?
When someone breaks the pencil lead,
          why do I get the blame?
When the newspaper gets lost,
          why do I have to find it again?

      I can answer all these questions.

    Because I broke the vase
    Because I made the garden untidy
    Because I ripped the book
    Because I broke the pencil lead
    Because I lost the paper.

                            Ben Bruton

Who are We?

There were these two snakes
crawling along the road
and one said:
'Are we the kind of snakes
that strangle people
or the kind of snakes
that bite people?'
And the other snake said:
'We're the kind of snakes
that strangle people.'
And the other snake said:
'That's good,
because I've just bit my lip.'

Anon

Your Photo

I wish I had your photo
it'd be very nice
I would put it up in the attic
to scare away the mice.

Anon

Dance Songs

Winter

Gently, gently,
gently, gently,
there away in the east,
the rain clouds are caring
for the little shoots of corn
like a mother takes care of her baby.

Flower Dance

Butterfly, butterfly,
butterfly, butterfly,
Oh look,
see it hovering among the flowers.
It's like a baby trying to walk
and not knowing how to go.
The clouds sprinkle down the rain.

Anon (The Acoma People,
south-west USA)

Sweet and Low

Sweet and low, sweet and low,
   Wind of the western sea,
Low, low, breathe and blow,
   Wind of the western sea!
Over the rolling waters go,
Come from the dying moon, and blow,
   Blow him again to me;
While my little one, while my pretty one sleeps.

Sleep and rest, sleep and rest,
   Father will come to thee soon;
Rest, rest, on mother's breast,
   Father will come to thee soon;
Father will come to his babe in the nest,
Silver sails all out of the west
   Under the silver moon;
Sleep, my little one, sleep, my pretty one, sleep.

Alfred Lord Tennyson

It's Very Nice

It's very nice
lying in Mama's bed
feeling
her soft breast
'gainst your hand
or your ear

Siv Widerberg

Fair Rosie

Fair Rosie was a lovely girl,
A lovely girl, a lovely girl,
Fair Rosie was a lovely girl,
A lovely girl.

Her ancient castle was her home,
Was her home, was her home,
Her ancient castle was her home,
Was her home.

Fair Rosie sat in her high tower,
Her high tower, her high tower,
Fair Rosie sat in her high tower,
Her high tower.

A wicked fairy found her there,
Found her there, found her there,
A wicked fairy found her there,
Found her there.

Fair Rosie slept a hundred years,
A hundred years, a hundred years,
Fair Rosie slept a hundred years,
A hundred years.

A handsome prince came riding by,
Riding by, riding by,
A handsome prince came riding by,
Riding by.

Fair Rosie did not sleep no more,
Sleep no more, sleep no more,
Fair Rosie did not sleep no more,
Sleep no more.

All the guests made merry there,
Merry there, merry there,
All the guests made merry there,
Merry there.

Anon

Dr Knickerbocker

Doctor Knickerbocker, Knickerbocker number nine,
Loves to dance to the rhythm of time.
Now let's get the rhythm of the hands
    CLAP CLAP
Now we've got the rhythm of the hands
    CLAP CLAP
Now let's get the rhythm of the feet
    STAMP STAMP
Now we've got the rhythm of the feet
    STAMP STAMP

Now let's get the rhythm of the eyes
    WIPE WIPE
Now we've got the rhythm of the eyes
    WIPE WIPE
Now let's get the rhythm of the dance
    WIGGLE WIGGLE
Now we've got the rhythm of the dance
    WIGGLE WIGGLE
    CLAP CLAP,
    STAMP STAMP,
    WIPE WIPE,
    WIGGLE WIGGLE
Now we're dancing to the rhythm of time,
Doctor Knickerbocker,
    Knickerbocker number nine.

Anon

The Cupboard

I was in the dark cupboard
all alone
sitting on the washing basket.
I switched the torch on
and I put my shadowed hand
on the ceiling.
My hand was so big
it was nearly as big as the cupboard.

Kevin Wright

The Shed

There's a shed at the bottom of our garden
With a spider's web hanging across the door,
The hinges are rusty and creak in the wind.
When I'm in bed I lie and I listen,
I'll open that door one day.

There's a dusty old window around at the side
With three cracked panes of glass,
I often think there's someone staring at me
Each time that I pass,
I'll peep through that window one day.

My brother says there's a ghost in the shed
Who hides under the rotten floorboards,
And if I ever dare to set foot inside
He'll jump out and chop off my head,
But I'll take a peek one day.

I know that there isn't really a ghost,
My brother tells lies to keep the shed for his den;
There isn't anyone staring or making strange noises
And the spider has been gone from his web
  since I don't know when,
I'll go into that shed one day soon,

But not just yet. . . .

    Frank Flynn

Burp

Pardon me
for being so rude.
It was not me
it was my food.
It just came up
to say hallo.
Now it's gone
back down below.

Anon

The Author

Michael Rosen is a funny one
he's got a nose like a pickled onion
he's got a face like a squashed tomato
and feet like fried fish.

Anon

Index of Authors

Index of First Lines

Acknowledgements

For permission to reproduce copyright material, acknowledgement and thanks are due to the following:
Eleanor Farjeon and Michael Joseph for 'Waking Up' from *Silver Sand and Snow*; Günter Grass and Harcourt Brace Jovanovich, Inc. for 'Happiness' from *Selected Poems* by Günter Grass (English translation by Michael Hamburger, © 1966 Martin Secker and Warburg Ltd); Ian Serraillier and Puffin Books for 'The Rescue' from *I'll Tell You A Tale* (© 1973 and 1976); Macmillan Publishing Company, Harper & Row, Publishers, Inc. and Willard R. Trask for his translation of 'Eskimo Lullaby' from *The Unwritten Song Vol. 1*, © 1966 Willard R. Trask, originally translated from *The Last Kings of Thule: A Year Among The Polar Eskimos of Greenland* by Jean Malaurie, translated by Gwendolen Freeman (T. Y. Crowell) © 1956 Harper & Row, Publishers, Inc; Macmillan Publishing Company for 'Praise Song of the Wind' from *The Unwritten Song, Vol. 2*, edited, with translations by Willard R. Trask © 1967 Willard R. Trask; V. Elwin and Allen and Unwin for an extract beginning 'The panther roars . . .' from *Songs of the Forest: The Folk Poetry of the Gonds*; Penguin Books and Lucien Stryk for his translation of 'One Bath' by Issa from *The Penguin Book of Zen Poetry*; Macmillan, London and Basingstoke, Macmillan Publishing Company, NY, and Rabindranath Tagore for 'The Wicked Postman' from *The Crescent Moon* in *Collected Poems and Plays of Rabindranath Tagore* (© 1913 Macmillan Publishing Company, renewed 1941 by Rabindranath Tagore); Michael Rosen for 'Two Pilots', 'Hey, Diddle, Diddle', 'Three Girls', 'London Bridge', 'My Mum Said', 'Little by Little', 'Man in a Hurry' and 'The Skyfoogle'; Joni Akinrele and Benthal Junior School for 'BED!'; Jay Reed and John Scurr Primary School for 'When I was Small'; Judith Nicholls and Faber and Faber Ltd for 'Space Shuttle' from *Magic Mirror and other poems for children* by Judith Nicholls; Annie Spike and Centerprise Trust Ltd for 'Office Cleaner'; Patricia Maria Tan and Educational Publications Bureau Pte Ltd, Singapore, for 'Into the Kitchen' from *Spot and I*; Phyllis Kingsbury for 'A Spider Bought a Bicycle'; A. A. Milne, Methuen Children's Books, E. P. Dutton (a division of NAL Penguin Inc.) and the Canadian publishers, McClelland and Stewart Ltd, Toronto, for 'The Good Little Girl' and 'Waiting at the Window' from *Now We Are Six* (© 1927 E. P. Dutton, renewed 1955 by A. A. Milne); James Reeves and Puffin Books for 'Cows' from *The Wandering Moon and Other Poems* (© James Reeves, reprinted by permission of the James Reeves Estate); Karla Kuskin and Harper and Row, Publishers, Inc. for 'When I Went Out' from *Dogs, Dragons, Trees and Dreams: A Collection of Poems by Karla Kuskin* (© Karla Kuskin); Edna St Vincent Millay and Harper and Row for 'Lament' from *Collected Poems* (© 1921, 1948 Edna St Vincent Millay, reprinted by permission of Elizabeth Barnett, literary executor); Ramona Harris and Centerprise Trust Ltd for 'The Day Our Dog Died' from *Stepney Words*; Langston Hughes and Alfred A. Knopf, Inc. for 'Dream Variations' from *Selected Poems of Langston Hughes* (© 1926 Alfred A. Knopf, inc., renewed 1954 by Langston Hughes); Dennis Lee, Macmillan of Canada (A Division of Canada Publishing Corporation) and Blackie and Son Ltd for 'The Gentle Giant' from *Jelly Belly* (© 1983 Dennis Lee); Elie Bagum and John Scurr Primary School for 'Tracy, our teacher . . .'; Jayne Spooner for 'The Underground Train'; Oxford University Press, Australia, for 'Hello, Sir' from *Far Out Brussel Sprout*, edited by June Factor; A. P. Watt Ltd on behalf of The Executors of the Estate of Robert Graves for 'Allie', from *Collected Poems 1975*; Ben Bruton and Wood's Foundation Church of England School for 'Why?'; Smithsonian Institution Press for two extracts from 'Dance Songs' entitled 'Flower Dance' and 'Winter' from *Music of the Acoma, Isleta, Cochiti and Zuni Pueblos* by Frances Densmore (Bureau of American Ethnology Bulletin 165. Smithsonian Institution, Washington, D.C. 1957); Siv Widerberg and The Feminist Press, City University of New York for 'It's Very Nice' from *I'm Like Me*, translated by Verne Moberg (© 1968, 1970, 1971 Siv Widerberg. Translation © 1973); Kevin Wright and Rushcroft School for 'The Cupboard'; Frank Flynn and Oxford University Press for 'The Shed' (© Frank Flynn 1984) from *The Candy-floss Tree*, poems by Gerda Mayer, Frank Flynn and Norman Nicholson (1984).

While every effort has been made to obtain permission, there may still be cases in which we have failed to trace a copyright holder. The publisher will be happy to correct any omission in future reprintings.